Orphans for the Czar

Orphans for the Czar

George F. Walker

Orphans for the Czar
first published 2023 by Scirocco Drama
An imprint of J. Gordon Shillingford Publishing Inc.
© 2023 George F. Walker

Scirocco Drama Editor: Glenda MacFarlane
Cover design by Doowah Design
Cover art: Russian peasant girl lapidary figurine by Peter Carl Fabergé,
circa 1910, held at The Met Museum, gift of R. Thornton Wilson,
in memory of Florence Ellsworth Wilson.
Author photo by Kate Walker
Production photos by Dahlia Katz for Crow's Theatre

Printed and bound in Canada on 100% post-consumer recycled paper.
We acknowledge the financial support of the Manitoba Arts Council and
The Canada Council for the Arts for our publishing program.

Production inquiries to:
Rena Zimmerman
Great North Artists Management Inc.
350 Dupont Street, Toronto, ON M5R 1V9
Toronto, Ontario, Canada
416-925-2051

Library and Archives Canada Cataloguing in Publication

Title: Orphans for the czar / George F. Walker.
Names: Walker, George F., author.
Description: A play.
Identifiers: Canadiana 20220492743 | ISBN 9781990738210 (softcover)
Classification: LCC PS8595.A557 O77 2023 | DDC C812/.54—dc23

J. Gordon Shillingford Publishing
P.O. Box 86, RPO Corydon Avenue, Winnipeg, MB Canada R3M 3S3

Suggested by

The Life of a Useless Man *by Maxim Gorky*

George F. Walker

George F. Walker is one of Canada's most prolific, decorated, and popular playwrights. Since beginning his theatre career in the early 1970s, Walker has written more than 30 plays, including *Suburban Motel*, *Love and Anger*, and *Nothing Sacred*. His plays have been translated into more than ten languages and have received many hundreds of productions around the world.

Foreword
By Tanja Jacobs

The best feeling you can get from a story is the secret pleasure of daydreaming about the lives of the characters after the story has ended. In George Walker's brilliant play, we ardently want the characters to find love, justice and lasting decency. Daylight floods in. We relive the selfless acts of these benighted Russians of 1905. Promise hovers over these beautiful young people, and then history interrupts. Through the viewfinder of the bloody twentieth century, we see what comes of their dreams of selfhood and freedom. Alas.

This poignant duality, of us on the one hand cheering for the orphans and dupes of Walker's chaotic world and on the other, thinking that if their long gaze finally met with ours, we would be looking back at them with pity; this 'one-two punch' is an essential aspect of George Walker's work as a playwright. It is his art. Comedy and Death enter, holding hands. The weak are clamorous. The language uttered by those in authority is lies. The world is treacherous, drop-chute sudden; it is subversive, it is explosively, pathetically funny.

In his works, Walker spotlights the rejected. These characters may appear at first invisible to those with power, but they then become a central problem to the powerful. Most often their intelligence is underestimated. If they are female, Walker will put them in situations where they communicate with directness and fly into action, almost always testing the limits of systems designed to keep them in line. Male characters will often bully instead of expressing their feelings of feebleness. In

George Walker's plays, death is real and often hapless. Dignity vaporizes. Deluded characters on the periphery commonly imagine they are the centre of the action and that they alone are responsible for things going to hell. Victory, such as it is, is achieved by people binding themselves to each other. The stakes are extremely high. The comedy, ballistic.

In *Orphans for the Czar*, it is Vasley Klimkov's weakness that becomes his strength. Having no social or political allegiances of any value, unacquainted with his own opinions on the hierarchy or social arrangements of his country, Vasley's survival relies on his wits. Filthy, ragged, sniping, beaten, his inability to decide what he thinks is intolerable to everyone. He's understood to have a deficit of sense, but his mind is of course quick and original. Even so, the lives of orphans are frail. "A child left to his own devices becomes a man without an anchor," Piotr explains to Rayisha. What is a man without an anchor? He is someone dead easy to corrupt.

In preparing a first production, details are needed. What did it mean to be poor in rural Russia? What of the famine that preceded the Bloody Sunday massacre? What about Russian childhood at the end of the 19th century? What did orphans endure? How do people live through the violent upheaval of an entire society? A timeline of the play's events was necessary, maps approximating distances between fictitious villages and St. Petersburg; questions asked about trains, bombs, horses, books, syphilis, pistols, prostitutes, spies, hunger, blindness. In the end, these details were fortifying but what actually led us through all of the scenes and their many locations was Walker's whirlwind logic, plus a simple, unifying design.

A director's most vital skill is recognizing when someone else's ideas are better than your own and incorporating them. Our production at Crow's Theatre was illuminated by many blazing minds at work. Chris Abraham, Crow's inspiring artistic director, must be acknowledged for his conviction to produce *Orphans for the Czar*.

Five days before rehearsal began, Russia invaded Ukraine. Volodymyr Zelensky, the short, Jewish, former comic actor swiftly emerged as Ukraine's valorous wartime leader. We were reminded daily of the lives of ordinary Russians, of the fact that Russia's rulers have always and forever lied to its people to justify theft, mutilation and killing.

Timothy Snyder, the Yale historian who has written extensively on Russia, recalls the definition of an ethical act proposed by the late Polish philosopher Leszek Kołakowski as "something which is more than anyone could have expected of you. And I think about that with respect to the Ukrainians over and over."

The ideas in Walker's play are purposeful. We might associate the notion of learning to think for oneself with the possibility of survival. Our catastrophic future will be here before anyone has figured out how to make us agree with each other. Somehow we must go forward without agreement. Maybe the only way we will tolerate the differences in each other is by learning to think for ourselves.

Tanja Jacobs is an award-winning actress and director. She directed the premiere production of Orphans for the Czar.

Production History

Orphans for the Czar premiered at Crow's Theatre, Toronto, Ontario, March 29–April 24, 2022.

Cast

Eric Peterson	Piotr / The Master
Christopher Allen	Yakov
Shayla Brown	Rayisha
Kyle Gatehouse	Sasha
Paolo Santalucia	Vasley
Patrick McManus	Makarov
Michelle Mohammed	Olga
Shauna Thompson	Maya

Creative Team

George F. Walker	Writer
Tanja Jacobs	Director
Lorenzo Savoini	Set Design
Ming Wong	Costume Design
Logan Cracknell	Lighting Design
Thomas Ryder Payne	Sound Design
Siobhan Richardson	Fight Director
Kat Chin	Stage Manager
Cristina Hernandez	Assistant Stage Manager
Farnoosh Talebpour	Apprentice Stage Manager
Laura Delchiaro	Head of Wardrobe
Lisa Nighswander	Head of Props

Rayisha (Shayla Brown) and Vasley (Paolo Santalucia) have a
conversation about the world. Crow's Theatre production, 2022.
Photo by Dahlia Katz.

Yakov (Christopher Allen) threatens Vasley (Paolo Santalucia).
Crow's Theatre production, 2022. Photo by Dahlia Katz.

Vasley (Paolo Santalucia) talks with Piotr (Eric Peterson). Crow's Theatre production, 2022. Photo by Dahlia Katz.

Olga (Michelle Mohammed) visits the bookstore and meets Vasley (Paolo Santalucia). Crow's Theatre production, 2022. Photo by Dahlia Katz.

Sasha (Kyle Gatehouse) and Makharov (Patrick McManus) with
Vasley (Paolo Santalucia). Crow's Theatre production, 2022. Photo
by Dahlia Katz.

Yakov (Christopher Allen), Maya (Shauna Thompson), Rayisha
(Shayla Brown) and Olga (Michelle Mohammed) are caught in the
riot. Crow's Theatre production, 2022. Photo by Dahlia Katz.

Vasley (Paolo Santalucia) and Yakov (Christopher Allen). Crow's Theatre production, 2022. Photo by Dahlia Katz.

Vasley (Paolo Santalucia) and The Master (Eric Peterson) in the bookshop. Crow's Theatre production, 2022. Photo by Dahlia Katz.

Persons

Vasley (early 20)

Rayisha (late teens)

Yakov (late 20)

*Piotr (50-ish)

*Master (")

Olga (20)

Maya (23)

Sasha (late 20s)

Makarov (40)

*They can (should?) be doubled.

Intermission is optional.

Scene 1

1905. A small Russian village near St. Petersburg. VASLEY (21) and RAYISHA (17) sit on a makeshift bench. She is blind. He is unkempt. And he has an open book on his lap.

RAYISHA: Why did you stop? Is it getting too dark to read?

VASLEY: No I can still see.

RAYISHA: Well please keep going then.

VASLEY: So you were enjoying it?

RAYISHA: I was curious about what was going to happen next.

VASLEY: And you cared?

RAYISHA: Yes. Didn't you?

VASLEY: Not at all.

RAYISHA: You didn't find the people in the story interesting? They were so different from all of us here.

VASLEY: In what way?

RAYISHA: Well they had money.

VASLEY: Yes. But how were they different?

RAYISHA: The money made them different.

VASLEY: In what way

RAYISHA: Vasley. Stop. You always do this.

VASLEY: I'm just asking questions.

RAYISHA: Yes. But why? I mean your questions don't always seem to have a purpose.

VASLEY: I'm sorry. I'll work on that.

> *YAKOV walks past them with an animal carcass on his shoulders. He thinks about stopping to say something but decides to keep walking.*

RAYISHA: That was Yakov?

VASLEY: Yes.

RAYISHA: I smelled blood.

VASLEY: He killed a small deer.

RAYISHA: I've heard there aren't many deer left.

VASLEY: It's true. We're all probably going to starve to death.

RAYISHA: A whole village starving to death. Who would allow that to happen?

VASLEY: Who would stop it?

RAYISHA: Do you think Yakov will share the meat from his kill?

VASLEY: Not with me.

RAYISHA: That's true. Why does he dislike you so much?

VASLEY:	He doesn't dislike me any more than the other boys do. He just hits the hardest.
RAYISHA:	But does them all disliking you make you sad?
VASLEY:	Many things make me sad. You for example.
RAYISHA:	Because I'm blind.
VASLEY:	Because you're blind and poor.
RAYISHA:	I'm no poorer than you are.
VASLEY:	But there's a small chance I might not always be poor. While you...
RAYISHA:	Will never be able to see.
VASLEY:	No. *(Looks at her, thinks.)* But that makes you lucky in a way. You'll never have to see how ugly the world really is.
RAYISHA:	My mother told me the world is beautiful.
VASLEY:	She was lying.
RAYISHA:	Why would she do that?
VASLEY:	She probably thought it would make you feel better. But it just made you feel worse, didn't it.
RAYISHA:	Well it made me sad that I couldn't—
VASLEY:	See it for yourself. Yes. Your mother was a heartless fool. But I'm going to tell you the truth about the world, and then you'll feel much better about not having to look at it. I'll start with the sky.
RAYISHA:	Mother told me it's bright blue.

VASLEY:	So what? You don't even know what blue is! Bright or otherwise. Not that it matters, because the sky is almost never bright blue. It's usually a dull dirty grey which after a while makes people want to kill themselves. You're lucky you can't see it. And you're lucky you don't have to look at the people in this village either. They all have hollow empty eyes. Crooked noses. Dirty blistered faces.
RAYISHA:	Including you?
VASLEY:	Well I've never had the courage to look at myself in the mirror. But I assume so.
RAYISHA:	And what about me?
VASLEY:	Well...you're the exception. You're very beautiful. It's a miracle because your mother's ugliness is what's made her so bitter.
RAYISHA:	She's not bitter. Her voice is sweet and full of love.
VASLEY:	Sweet loving voices are all that mothers have to offer now. They can't feed us properly or save us when we're very ill. And they usually die early and leave us in horrible circumstances.
RAYISHA:	Like yours did.
VASLEY:	Yes. But at least I don't have to look at her anymore. I'm telling you there's nothing but ugliness all around you. In the people, in the sky, even in the animals. All the animals who haven't already starved to death have sunken terrified eyes. Skin sagging from their bones. Trust me, Rayisha. You're very lucky that you can't see them. Or anything else.

RAYISHA: No. That can't be—

VASLEY: It's true! It is!

RAYISHA: *(Crying.)* No. It's not. It can't be!

She starts off, stumbles and falls. VASLEY tries to help her up.

No. Leave me alone. *(Pushing him away.)* Leave me!

She gets up. Rushes off, almost bumping into YAKOV on his way in.

YAKOV: Whoa there.

He corrects her course and pushes her gently off.

If she stays steadily in that direction she should make it home okay.

VASLEY: Very generous of you to give her a good push though.

YAKOV: What did you do to her? You didn't hurt her? Or touch her in some way?

VASLEY: You mean in a way that you would have.

YAKOV: *(Advancing.)* It's because you say things like that—

VASLEY: That you beat me so often?

YAKOV: What trouble did you just cause Rayisha?

VASLEY: She's sad about being blind. So I tried to make her feel better about it.

YAKOV: By upsetting her.

VASLEY: For now. But what I said could help her in the long run. Do you want to know what it was?

YAKOV: I think I'll have to beat you for whatever it was.

VASLEY: Okay. But wait a day or two. If you let yesterday's bruises heal, imagine how much you'll enjoy giving me a few new ones.

YAKOV: How many times do I have to tell you? I don't beat you for enjoyment. I'm trying to knock some sense into you.

VASLEY: I think it's probably a little of both. So please just get on with it. My aunt will be waiting for me to clean up after their supper.

YAKOV: Their supper? Your uncle still can't convince her to let you eat with them?

VASLEY: She says the sight of me turns her stomach.

YAKOV: Well maybe if you bathed occasionally things would be better for you.

VASLEY: I'm an orphan. Things are exactly how they're supposed to be for me. So are you going to beat me or not?

YAKOV: No. You've ruined the mood.

VASLEY: Then if you'll excuse me... *(A mocking bow.)* I'll be on my way.

                        VASLEY starts off.

YAKOV: Vasley.

VASLEY: *(Stopping.)* Yes?

YAKOV: Rayisha has enough to worry about without you making her listen to all the strange things that come out of your mouth.

                        VASLEY leaves. YAKOV just watches him go.

Scene 2

> *VASLEY is dragged on by his Uncle PIOTR holding his ear. PIOTR is wearing a blacksmith's apron. And holding a poker.*

PIOTR: Everyone's suspicious about what you did to upset that girl.

VASLEY: Yes. I might have gone too far.

PIOTR: You mean you touched her? For godsake. There's an agreement that men should never touch her.

VASLEY: Just because she's blind?

PIOTR: Well would you like to be touched if you were blind?

VASLEY: Wouldn't that depend on who was doing the touching?

PIOTR: So you did touch her! *(Grabs his crotch.)* I piss on your mother's grave!

VASLEY: What's she got to do with it?

PIOTR: I thought you were a decent boy. But you're just as disgusting as all the rest of them.

VASLEY: No they're much worse! And I didn't—

> *PIOTR whips him a little with the apron's leather wrap.*

PIOTR: I should beat you to death right here! You wanna say a prayer first, or should I get right to it?!

VASLEY: *(Cowering.)* No! Please! I didn't touch her. I... just described something to her!

PIOTR: You did what?

VASLEY: Not that! I described the world to her...in a way that would make her feel better about being blind. I made her believe it was ugly.

PIOTR: Ugly. The whole world?

VASLEY: Yes.

PIOTR: Well who the hell are you to be doing something like that.

VASLEY: I think it helped her.

PIOTR: Idiot. How could that help her. It probably made her feel worse about even being alive.

VASLEY: Good point. Sometimes I have these thoughts that I don't completely understand myself.

PIOTR: Then here's some advice. Stop thinking. Let other people do it for you.

VASLEY: All right. But maybe other people should also try to help Rayisha instead of just letting her bump into things. Or wander off and get lost in the woods.

PIOTR: She doesn't do that as much as she used to.

VASLEY: She did it this evening. That's where I found her.

PIOTR: Oh. All right. I can spread the word. Have the villagers keep more of an eye on her. But you made a mistake, telling her all that about the world. And I'm sure the general opinion will be that you should be beaten for it.

VASLEY: By who?

PIOTR: Anyone who wants to. I'd do it myself if I thought it would be of any use. But beatings don't help someone like you.

VASLEY: Is a beating supposed to help? Isn't causing pain the only point?

PIOTR: I'm too tired to continue this conversation. Talking to you is exhausting!

VASLEY: I've heard that mentioned.

PIOTR: Well here's another idea that will help you get through life more easily. Stop talking altogether. If you find that too hard, do it gradually. And eventually just mostly listen. And watch more. Right now, in fact. (*Leaving.*) Just watch me hammer that horseshoe and try to learn something.

VASLEY: (*Following.*) Who is it for?

PIOTR: (*Stopping.*) Someone with a horse.

VASLEY: No one in this village owns a horse anymore.

PIOTR: Someone might pass through.

VASLEY: What was for supper?

PIOTR: Root vegetables and chicken fat. We saved you some.

VASLEY: You mean you did. Your wife doesn't care if I ever eat again.

PIOTR: Well none of us will be eating for much longer if we don't get help. No one seems to know we even exist. (*An idea.*) How about you doing something useful for once. Take yourself to Petersburg and spread our story.

VASLEY: You mean talk about it.

PIOTR: Yes. But nothing else, all right. And find someone to tell the Czar how hard up we are.

VASLEY: The whole county is hard up. Does the Czar care?

PIOTR: He says he does. But he's a disgusting liar. And I'd like to shove this poker up his ass. When you get there make a big fuss about our situation. Maybe we can shame him. Weep and tell everyone our crops have failed, most of the livestock have died, and the people are losing their will to live. Now go prepare to leave.

VASLEY: By doing what? I've never left anywhere before.

PIOTR: Oh for godsake.

VASLEY: Then there's the getting to somewhere. I've never done that either. Where am I going to stay? Winter is coming, and I'm not healthy enough to survive on the street.

PIOTR: I know someone who could put you up. He's my half-brother, or so he says. The man isn't as easygoing as me, so you might have to let him kick you around from time to time.

VASLEY: *(Leaving.)* Of course.

PIOTR: *(Following.)* I'm not sure about that. I'm just saying be prepared!

VASLEY: *(To himself.)* Of course...

Scene 3

*Bookshop. Sloppy piles of books and a cot
in the corner. VASLEY enters, stands there
and looks around.*

VASLEY: Hello. Hello! Is anyone here?!

The MASTER is just a voice from upstairs.

MASTER: Yes! I'm here!

VASLEY: Oh. Well... Hello!

MASTER: Yes yes, hello. Are you the boy my cousin
sent?

VASLEY: You mean your half-brother.

MASTER: If he says so. So you're here then. You actually
came.

VASLEY: Yes. I came. I'm here.

MASTER: Good. So you can get right to work then.

VASLEY: Yes. Doing what?

MASTER: This is a bookshop.

VASLEY: Yes. I see.

MASTER: *(Head in the light.)* You see. And do you see if
the books look ready to sell?

VASLEY: They're in piles. Are you selling them in
piles?

MASTER: No of course not. They were being sorted
into categories. I was in the process of doing
it when I fell ill. So that's your first task.

VASLEY: And that would be a useful thing for me to
do?

MASTER: Well why else would I ask you to do it? I was told you could read.

VASLEY: Yes. I read well.

The MASTER starts down into the room but can't make it all the way and lets himself settle on a step. He looks like PIOTR, but more decrepit. And he has several open sores on his face.

MASTER: *(Breathing a touch heavily.)* That's nothing to brag about. They're teaching most people to read these days. Well not in the villages. That might be too dangerous. They read. They learn. They revolt. But in the cities they're hoping it will make the wheels of commerce turn more quickly. Where was I?

VASLEY: You asked if I could read.

MASTER: Yes. And you can, so you should have no problem with the task then. Alphabetical order by title in groups of similar content. History. Agriculture. The Law. And so on.

VASLEY: Is there a wage?

MASTER: Perhaps. Eventually. But for now there's just room and board.

VASLEY: Okay. So...where is it?

MASTER: Where's what?

VASLEY: My room.

MASTER: That was just an expression. You'll sleep on that cot. Are you content with that?

VASLEY: If that's what it is, then that's what it is.

MASTER: Spoken like a true Russian peasant. Or a thoughtless dictator. Later a woman will arrive and cook us supper. We'll eat up above because, as you saw, the stairs are difficult for me.

VASLEY: (A chuckle.) And that was just coming down.

MASTER: (A look.) Right. Now I have some questions for you. After you've answered them you can get to work. These are questions meant to determine if you'll be able to remain impartial about the material we sell here. Are you ready?

VASLEY: Yes. No. No, yes.

MASTER: Good God. What's wrong with you?

VASLEY: Nothing. Not really. I sometimes have problems with questions like that.

MASTER: I haven't asked a question yet.

VASLEY: You asked if I was ready. And right away I started thinking about all the ways I might not be, and then—

MASTER: Here's the first actual question. Do you have strong feelings? Opinions. Passionate opinions. About anything?

VASLEY: No.

MASTER: Well you answered that very quickly.

VASLEY: Well the fact that I have no strong feelings about anything is really the one thing I know for certain about myself.

MASTER: Are you sure? What about the overall condition of the population, for example.

VASLEY: You mean the poor?

MASTER: That's what I just said.

VASLEY: You said the population.

MASTER: And isn't the population by and large poor?

VASLEY: I'm not sure.

MASTER: You aren't. Well then here's some news for you. They fucking are!! And now that you know that, do you care?

VASLEY: I'm not in a position to care about anyone except myself. Maybe I would if I had time and sufficient comfort to consider all the—

MASTER: But moving on. Do you have strong opinions about the church?

VASLEY: No. But I like to sing hymns.

MASTER: Because...

VASLEY: Of how it makes me feel.

MASTER: Which is?

VASLEY: Both very big and very small.

MASTER: At the same time?

VASLEY: Yes.

MASTER: Interesting. What about God. I ask that separately from the church question because they're not the same thing.

VASLEY: I don't know about God.

MASTER: Do you mean you don't believe in God?

VASLEY: No, I mean I don't know anything about God including whether I believe in him or not.

MASTER:	Talking to you is making me very tired. I'm sure you have that effect on most people. So just get to work and do your best for now.

The MASTER starts back up the stairs.

VASLEY:	What about the prices? Are they written in the books.
MASTER:	Of course not. That would be outrageously vulgar.
VASLEY:	Oh. But when they want a book how am I to know what to charge them?
MASTER:	You don't charge them anything. When they want a book they usually pay what they think it's worth.
VASLEY:	Suppose they don't think it's worth anything.
MASTER:	Why would they want a book they didn't think was worth anything? Listen, let them take it no matter what they say about it. Unless you want to get into a fist fight about it.
VASLEY:	Suppose they pay for the book and after they've read it, they decide it's worth less than they paid for it, or even worth nothing. Should I give them all or part of their money back?
MASTER:	Well that would be carrying it a bit far.
VASLEY:	So no refunds then. But also no fist fights. I think I've got it.
MASTER:	What's your name again?
VASLEY:	Vasley. Vasley Klimkov.

MASTER: (*Stops and turns.*) You're a puzzle, aren't you Vasley Klimkov. The impression you've given from this short conversation is that you're both somewhat intelligent and also in many ways very very stupid. What do the people back in your village think about you.

VASLEY: Oh. I'm pretty sure they think I'm just stupid.

MASTER: (*Heading all the way back to his room.*) Well as long as you're here, try not to prove them right.

VASLEY: I will.

> He starts to look through the piles of books.

Scene 4

> Bookshop. Later. VASLEY is asleep on the cot. OLGA is browsing through the piles. Finds a book. Starts to look through it. Something in it makes her laugh. VASLEY stirs. Sits up. Sees her. Flops back down.

OLGA: Oh. Sorry. I didn't mean to wake you.

VASLEY: You laughed.

OLGA: Ah... Yes I did.

VASLEY: At me?

OLGA   No.

VASLEY: It's all right. I'm used to it.

OLGA: But I wasn't— People laugh at you so much that you've gotten used to it?

VASLEY: Well what other choice do I have?

OLGA:	No I mean why do they— Anyway I wasn't laughing at you. Something in this book reminded me of—
VASLEY:	*(Straining to see.)* It's in French. Do you read French?
OLGA:	Of course. *(Chuckling.)* Or how could I have— I'm sorry.
VASLEY:	For what?
OLGA:	For what I said. Or maybe how I said it. I could tell it bothered you.
VASLEY:	If it bothered me, I would have said it bothered me. Which it did. But not enough to say it did.
OLGA:	Do you mind if I give you a little advice?
VASLEY:	*(Staring at her.)* What? Oh. Yes. I mean no. I'd be honoured to receive anything from you. Advice or even... severe criticism.
OLGA:	*(An odd look.)* Oh. Well I was just going to suggest that if you thought a little before you spoke then— Look you can go back to sleep if you like. I'll just continue to browse.
VASLEY:	No.
OLGA:	I can't browse?
VASLEY:	I can't sleep. I'm in charge of these books.
OLGA:	Since when?
VASLEY:	Today. The Master has fallen ill.
OLGA:	I know. I'm a regular customer. I usually just come in, look around and leave money for whatever I take. You call him Master?

VASLEY: I shouldn't?

OLGA: He's your employer. Not your owner.

VASLEY: Well if he ever starts paying me I'll start using his name.

OLGA: He doesn't pay you anything?

VASLEY: He says he might eventually.

OLGA: Do you want me to have a word with him about that?

VASLEY: What would that word be?

OLGA: I'll appeal to his sense of fair play. I know he has one. I've been coming here since I started university.

VASLEY: Oh. University. They allow women? *(Off her look.)* I mean of course they do.

OLGA: I'm sure most of the professors don't like it, but—

VASLEY: What's wrong with him? My... employer. What illness does he have?

OLGA: Syphilis... *(Off his look.)* The pox?

VASLEY: Oh.

OLGA: You haven't seen him?

VASLEY: Not clearly. He stays mostly in the darkness.

OLGA: Well then you better prepare yourself. He's not actually disfigured yet. But there are some open sores on his face.

VASLEY: Open sores. I might not react well to that.

OLGA: That kind of thing offends you, does it?

VASLEY:	No. But it sometimes amuses me. (*Off her look.*) I mean if I get caught off-guard my responses aren't always...correct.
OLGA:	I see. Well anyway, now that you know, you can prepare yourself... (*Hands him several coins.*) Here. For the book.
VASLEY:	This is a lot of money. I mean for something that's not food or clothing.
OLGA:	I hear it's worth it.
VASLEY:	What's it about?
OLGA:	It's about how to change the world.
VASLEY:	All of it.
OLGA:	One place at a time. But yes, eventually the entire world.

She starts out.

VASLEY:	Will you be coming back anytime soon?
OLGA:	Probably. (*Stops.*) And when I do, will you be looking at me the same way you are now?
VASLEY:	I don't...
OLGA:	You're very young. But even so, the way you look at me is...actually quite...
VASLEY:	Annoying?
OLGA:	No. Just a little...

She smiles. Leaves. He just watches her go. Eyes wide open.

VASLEY:	A little what? (*Towards the door.*) A little what?!

Scene 5

> *MAKAROV waits under a street light. He checks his watch. Looks at us.*

MAKAROV: I seem to have some time on my hands, so let me tell you a little about what's going on. It's 1905 and Russia has fallen into a pit of despair. The people, as usual, are hungry, angry, confused, vulnerable and deeply apprehensive. Not all of us of course. Some of us have sufficient resources to withstand most of the chaos and terror that's about to erupt and therefore don't actually care that much about it at all. But the people in general, let's call them all peasants... because that best describes their unmatched ignorance about anything beyond their limited vision, and also to some degree, their odour. The "peasants" have recently decided that they have definitely and even passionately had enough! Having been driven, ironically, to that conclusion by not having enough. Not enough food. Not enough land. Not enough hope. And not nearly enough power to get more food or land...or not enough knowledge to even understand what hope, power, and knowledge really are. And they know of course that eventually there will be some kind of war in which most of them will be callously sacrificed. So...they are now in the process of turning into not much more than vermin that sniff and scratch at the ground or wild beasts that howl pathetically in the darkness. Unthinking, unknowing, looking for any form of comfort, ready to be led by anyone who needs, for their own self-gratification, to have a crowd following behind and applauding every idiotic utterance.

Anyone who knows a few rhetorical tricks that can hypnotize the ignorant and bend them to his will. Tricks and lies about faulty ideologies. And even on occasion their sexual prowess. These "anyones," these violence-prone men and newly-educated women, their heads full of romantic foreign ideas, have made themselves "leaders" of the coming insurrection. And it's them who need to be watched. Constantly. And very closely. Which is what I do. And do very well. That is, when I can find enough people with half a brain to help me out.

SASHA approaches.

Ah. Here comes half a brain now.

SASHA: Good evening, brother.

MAKAROV: You're late. And don't call me brother.

SASHA: I'm sorry. I can't help feeling a certain kinship with you.

MAKAROV: I'm your boss. There is no kinship. There are only my orders and your obedience. For example, when I tell you to be at a certain place at a certain time—

SASHA: I was on duty.

MAKAROV: You mean you were watching that doctor?

SASHA: Yes.

MAKAROV: So where was he?

SASHA: At home.

MAKAROV: And how long had he been there?

SASHA: Several hours.

MAKAROV: Did he have any visitors?

SASHA: No.

MAKAROV: Was the house still lit?

SASHA: No. All dark.

MAKAROV: So you were watching a man asleep in his own bed then.

SASHA: Well yes maybe. Now that you—

MAKAROV: And you were so intent on that task that you forgot you had a place to be. Someone to meet. Or did you fall asleep yourself, leaning against a fence perhaps?

SASHA: You saw?

MAKAROV: No.

SASHA: You were told then.

MAKAROV: No. I neither saw nor was told.

SASHA: Then it was just a lucky guess. Good for you. But that's never gonna happen again, Boss.

MAKAROV: Meaning what? That you won't fall asleep on the job or that you won't let me trick you into admitting it?

SASHA: Both. I mean either one. But mostly the first one. No more sleeping. I mean when I shouldn't be. But here's the thing, I was very tired and—

MAKAROV: Shh. I'm going to tell you something, and now that you're refreshed from your nap, I'm hoping you'll be able to take in all I say and remember it very clearly.

SASHA: Absolutely.

MAKAROV: I need you to be better. Things are happening very quickly, and we need more information if we want to be prepared for all that's coming.

SASHA: I couldn't agree more.

MAKAROV: Your agreement is another example of something I don't require. Just pay attention to what I'm saying. You need more sources. Many more. And much better ones.

SASHA: Yes. All right. And how should I find them?

MAKAROV: You're not expected to find them. We'll find them. You'll manage them.

SASHA: Sure. But suppose I find one myself.

MAKAROV: Well if by some miracle you pull that off then—

SASHA: That will be a feather in my cap?

MAKAROV: A very small feather. Nothing to brag about. But in the meantime there's a bookshop. People that we need to know more about often go there.

SASHA: Why?

MAKAROV: To get books.

SASHA: Of course. But for what other reason, is what I think I'm asking.

MAKAROV: There is no other reason, Sasha. Everything these people need to know about, and what to think about what they know about, is in those books. They are full of dangerous subversive thinking and we, the Czar's agents, need to know more about them.

SASHA: The books?

MAKAROV: The people.

SASHA: And the books?

MAKAROV: No! Just the people! We need to know who buys these books that recommend upsetting the established order. And that means you need to make contact and recruit the owner of this shop. Can you do that?

SASHA: Is there money in the budget for a healthy bribe?

MAKAROV: Yes. But first apply pressure.

SASHA: You mean threats.

MAKAROV: Clearly. And if those don't work use force.

SASHA: You mean a beating.

MAKAROV: Yes. But not too severe. And after that...if there is still resistance we'll find money to give him.

SASHA: Good. Because some of these merchants only respond to money.

MAKAROV: He's not a Jew if that's what you're implying.

SASHA: I was. And he's not?

MAKAROV: No. Not all merchants are Jews. Not all Jews are merchants. Not everyone who likes money is a Jew.

SASHA: Oh...

MAKAROV: Many of us have other concerns. Some of us are even spies.

SASHA: Oh. So...you're a Jew.

MAKAROV: Yes.

SASHA: And have I offended you?

MAKAROV: Yes.

SASHA: And... will I be punished for that?

MAKAROV: *(As he leaves.)* Eventually.

> *SASHA tries to light a cigarette, but he is too nervous to bring the match to the cigarette and eventually gives up.*

Scene 6

> *Bookshop. OLGA and her slightly older sister MAYA are browsing through the piles. Some of which are now spread on the floor. MAYA has short cropped hair and wears trousers and boots. VASLEY can't take his eyes off OLGA, who is piling the books she wants in his arms.*

OLGA: Do you think you'll ever manage to get these organized?

VASLEY: Our cook quit. I've been busy taking care of the meals and some of the Master's other needs.

MAYA: It doesn't matter. I enjoy the randomness of it all.

OLGA: *(To VASLEY.)* What other needs?

VASLEY: I'm sorry?

OLGA: What else do you have to do for him?

MAYA: Stop pestering him.

OLGA: I want to know. *(To VASLEY.)* So?

VASLEY: I can't tell you.

OLGA: Is it a secret?

VASLEY: I don't know. But I can't tell you no matter what. *(Gestures to MAYA.)* I can tell...her.

OLGA: Why her and not me?

VASLEY: She looks more...

MAYA: *(To VASLEY.)* Like a man?

OLGA: Because...she's wearing pants?

VASLEY: Well that and—

MAYA: My hair.

VASLEY: Yes. Your hair.

OLGA: Oh. Good God. You know, if you weren't so ignorant you'd know that many women in Western Europe are—

MAYA: Olga. Shh.

OLGA: What's wrong? He knows he's ignorant. *(To VASLEY.)* Don't you?

VASLEY: Of course.

MAYA: It doesn't mean you can rub it in. It's not his fault that he hasn't been able to travel.

OLGA: You're right. *(To VASLEY.)* I'm sorry. I have a lot on my mind these days. We're planning... a large event.

MAYA goes to VASLEY. Leans in.

MAYA: Just whisper. What is it that you do for your "Master"?

VASLEY whispers in her ear.

Right. That's what I thought. *(Taking OLGA's pile from VASLEY.)* He procures for him.

She puts the pile on a table. And points at it for Olga. But OLGA is already turning on VASLEY.

OLGA: So you're not only ignorant. You're sickening.

MAYA: Olga. If he wants to keep his job, maybe he doesn't have a choice.

OLGA: There's always a choice. *(To MAYA.)* How often do you bring these poor women to him?

VASLEY: Every Monday.

OLGA: Today's Monday. Is there someone up there with him now?

MAYA: What's that to you?

OLGA: *(To VASLEY.)* Is there?

VASLEY: Not yet. I'll go for her when it gets dark.

OLGA: *(To MAYA.)* Because he doesn't want people to see her come in. *(To VASLEY.)* Are they actually women. Or are they more like girls?

VASLEY: When is a woman a girl?

OLGA: When she's under eighteen.

MAYA: Sixteen.

OLGA: No. Eighteen at least. Preferably twenty. *(To VASLEY.)* How old are they usually?

VASLEY: *(Chuckles a little.)* Definitely not twenty.

OLGA: Sickening! *(To MAYA.)* Did you hear that, Maya? They're still children.

MAYA: You just turned twenty yourself.

OLGA: But I was a mature adult by the time I was fifteen. I'm going up there to talk to him.

                         She starts off.

MAYA: Olga. Don't!

OLGA: *(To MAYA.)* Don't? That's it? Don't!? The old degenerate. And with his condition. *(To VASLEY.)* Does he warn them?

VASLEY: The ones I bring have it too. He has a list of them, and I—

OLGA: You go fetch them.

VASLEY: Well sometimes they're brought. Or they just show up. But mostly I go get them while the stew is simmering. Please, if you go up there he'll know I told you. And he'll beat me.

MAYA: Does he beat you often?

VASLEY: Never. But I'm sure this would change that.

OLGA: *(To MAYA.)* This is just so wrong.

MAYA: Yes. But very common.

OLGA: And that should stop us from doing something about it?

MAYA: Only if it's something rash that might cause us to receive...unwanted attention.

                         She points to OLGA's pile.

             (To VASLEY.) We'll talk about this, and let you know how to proceed.

VASLEY: Do we really need to proceed? I might lose my job. Be thrown out on the street. Starve to death.

MAYA:	*(To OLGA.)* Is that what you want for him, Olga?
OLGA:	No. But he's still... *(She picks up her books, looks at VASLEY.)* Very disappointing.

MAYA hangs back.

VASLEY:	Well at least now I'm just disappointing. I don't think I could stand being sickening. I mean not to her. I mean...
MAYA:	*(Smiles.)* I understand. She smiles. Men fall in love. She gets a bit harsh. They stay in love. *(She starts out, stops.)* Just to warn you, your situation here might never change. We probably won't come up with a satisfactory solution. We haven't come up with one to anything else so far.

She leaves just as SASHA is entering.

SASHA:	Who were they?
VASLEY:	Who are you?

SASHA hits him in the face. He falls back into a pile of books. Some of them spill off.

SASHA:	Your new boss.
MASTER:	*(From above.)* What the hell is going on down there!
SASHA:	Tell him it's nothing.
VASLEY:	*(Yelling up.)* Nothing. Everything is fine.
MASTER:	*(From above.)* I'm getting hungry! Did you hear me?!
SASHA:	Tell him yes.
VASLEY:	Yes! I heard you. I'll start supper soon!

SASHA:	But first you need to do something. Tell him.
VASLEY:	*(To MASTER.)* I have to do something first!
MASTER:	What?!
VASLEY:	*(To SASHA.)* What?
SASHA:	You need to listen. I'm going to tell you what I want you to do and where I want you to go. And you need to listen to me very closely, okay.
MASTER:	So what is it then. What do you need to do?! Answer me, dammit!
SASHA:	Okay that's enough of this.

SASHA rushes up the stairs. Heads in.

MASTER:	What is this? Who are you?!
SASHA:	No more questions!!

A slap. A groan.

MASTER:	All right. *(Whimpers.)* But...who are you?

Another slap. Another groan. A whimper.

SASHA:	I said no more questions! Now be quiet, and let me finish my discussion with your clerk!

SASHA hurries down the stairs.

Now where were we?

SASHA approaches VASLEY.

VASLEY:	*(Takes a step.)* I was here. *(Points.)* And you were over there.

SASHA looks at him, puzzled. Gets closer, looks at him more closely.

SASHA: Are you being clever with me?

VASLEY: No, sir.

SASHA: Okay. So I'll ask you again. Where were we?

VASLEY: Well I was definitely just here. But you might have been closer to the—

>   *SASHA hits him again, and VASLEY collapses.*

SASHA: *(Leaning over him.)* Ready to listen now?

Scene 7

>   *MAKAROV waits at a table in a tavern. SASHA enters.*

MAKAROV: Where is he?

SASHA: He's coming. He had to make excuses to the owner.

MAKAROV: The owner, yes. He should be the one your boy reports on most regularly.

SASHA: Because?

MAKAROV: Of his profession. Books are a kind of lechery. They excite imagination. Create useless agitation. That's our official position on the subject, by the way.

SASHA: Our position on...books.

MAKAROV: Yes.

>   *SASHA takes out a pad.*

What's that for?

SASHA: I think I should be writing this down. These things you tell me could prove to be useful.

MAKAROV: Even though you don't actually understand them.

SASHA: I meant useful for me to say to other recruits. To keep them from...

MAKAROV: From what?

SASHA   Reading?

MAKAROV: Good. All right then. Write this down as well. Books used to be valuable when they were about history. But new books inspire hostility towards life. Imagination destroys faith.

SASHA: And causes agitation. *(Off his look.)* That's what you said once before about imagination. That it causes—

MAKAROV: So you have a half decent memory. A good memory can sometimes compensate for low intelligence.

SASHA: I'll remember that.

MAKAROV: Fine. As long as you don't try to explain it. And promise me you'll never read a book. Especially one of these new ones.

            (To audience.) Only old people should be allowed to read these new books. Because after a certain age the experience you have protects you from the discord and violence they propose. No one over fifty wants to live through more upheaval.

SASHA: Is that why they hurry up and die?

MAKAROV: I'm over fifty. Do I seem impatient to meet my end?

SASHA: You're different.

MAKAROV: Yes. Because I dream constantly about a better life.

                VASLEY is entering. There is a large bruise on his face. MAKAROV looks at SASHA.

                Is that him?

SASHA: Yes.

MAKAROV: What a pathetic creature.

SASHA: Too pathetic to be of use?

MAKAROV: Absolutely not. You looked much the same when I found you.

SASHA: I'm pretty sure I didn't slouch so much. *(To VASLEY.)* Well come sit down. Why are you just standing there?

                MAKAROV gestures to VASLEY in a friendly manner. VASLEY still hesitates a little.

MAKAROV: What happened to his face?

SASHA: I hit him.

MAKAROV: Why?

SASHA: To establish my authority. Just like you did to me.

MAKAROV: You were insolent. And full of yourself. This man is already somewhat broken. Never do it again.

                VASLEY is at their table. He sits.

                So you were able to get away.

VASLEY: My boss is busy right now.

MAKAROV: With a customer?

VASLEY: No. She might take a book with her... after they're done. But only to sell. I don't think she can read.

MAKAROV: Done doing what?

VASLEY: What they do. Or what he does to her. I don't really know what that is.

MAKAROV: Would you like me to tell you?

VASLEY: No thank you.

SASHA: You can tell me.

VASLEY: Yes. Or later, I might actually show you.

SASHA: *(To VASLEY.)* Do you want something to drink?

VASLEY: No.

SASHA: Thank you.

VASLEY: For what?

SASHA: Don't just say "no" to him. Say "no thank you."

MAKAROV: That's not necessary. *(To VASLEY.)* Do you know why you're here?

VASLEY: He told me I had to come or I'd get a lot more... *(Points to bruise.)* ...of this

MAKAROV: He was wrong. I assure you he'll never say or do anything like that to you again.

SASHA: Unless he deserves it. Like I did.

MAKAROV: Which I know he won't. *(To SASHA.)* Wait outside.

SASHA: But suppose you say something I could maybe use later.

MAKAROV: You mean you might want to quote me.

SASHA: Not without your permission.

MAKAROV: Outside.

              MAKAROV just looks at him. SASHA nods, leaves.

              So you only came here to avoid a beating.

VASLEY: Yes. Unless I had another reason I'm not sure of right now.

MAKAROV: I'm sorry?

VASLEY: I sometimes do things for reasons that only become clear to me much later. Why did you want me here?

MAKAROV: To talk about a better job for yourself. A more important job.

VASLEY: You mean a job where I'd be useful in some way?

MAKAROV: You'd be helping your country.

VASLEY: Why would I want to do that?

MAKAROV: Don't you love your country?

VASLEY: No. Why would I?

MAKAROV: Because it's part of your life. It protects you.

VASLEY: From who?

MAKAROV: People from other countries who want to come here and steal our valuable resources. The Germans. The English. Do you know anything about those peoples?

VASLEY: I know that the Germans speak German. And the English speak English.

MAKAROV: And imagining that they invade us one day soon, do you have any desire to speak either of those languages?

VASLEY: I don't think about things like that.

MAKAROV: What do you think about?

VASLEY: Well for the last couple of years, food mostly. And also heat. When I get cold I think a lot about heat because I can never get enough of it.

MAKAROV: And the same with food? You don't get enough of that either?

VASLEY: Who does?

MAKAROV: I do. Would you like to have a job that assures that you never have to worry about getting enough food or heat ever again.

VASLEY: Is that the kind of job you're offering me?

MAKAROV: I'm not offering anything. We're just talking. I'm telling you things. You're listening. I'll eventually ask you questions. You'll try to answer them. I'll guide you if you're having difficulty.

            (*To audience.*) We'll proceed in that manner and eventually I'll come to a decision about his suitability. You'll find out how it went soon enough. In the meantime...

            (*To VASLEY.*) Do you want something to eat?

VASLEY: Do they serve anything here with meat in it?

MAKAROV: Everything here has meat in it.

VASLEY:	Then I'll have some, yes.
MAKAROV:	You'll have what exactly? The beef? The mutton? The pork?
VASLEY:	I have to choose? It's been so long since I've had any of those things.
MAKAROV:	Of course. I understand. You poor fellow.

MAKAROV raises his hand for service.

(To audience.) Pathetic? Yes. But he'll work out just fine.

Scene 8

> *The Village. PIOTR in his blacksmith apron sits on the bench beside RAYISHA who wears a mourning scarf.*

PIOTR:	It came on her suddenly, didn't it.
RAYISHA:	So many people are saying that to me.
PIOTR:	They just mean that it's good she didn't suffer.
RAYISHA:	Except that she did.
PIOTR:	But not for long. Some people suffer their entire lives, Rayisha. You, for example. You could be in for some difficult times now. Did your mother make arrangements for your care?
RAYISHA:	She never had time to do anything except keep us both alive.
PIOTR:	So how will you live?

RAYISHA: The priest suggested a convent.

PIOTR: That's all he could come up with, eh.

RAYISHA: Yes. And I hate that idea. I'd rather walk into the forest and let the wolves tear off my flesh.

PIOTR: Better you take whatever little the church has to offer.

RAYISHA: Can I stay with you and your wife?

PIOTR: My wife's been driven insane by the heartache of five stillbirths.

RAYISHA: I won't be any bother. I'll stay out of her way. And I can cook.

PIOTR: There's very little to eat, so that won't help your case. And even if she let you stay, eventually she'd do something really awful to you.

RAYISHA: Worse than the wolves?

PIOTR: I'd rather not find out. I think we should get you to Petersburg.

RAYISHA: Petersburg. No. I can't survive there.

PIOTR: Not on your own. But we'll try to get you set up somewhere. I'll send Yakov with you. He knows where Vasley is, and maybe between the two of them...

RAYISHA: Vasley scares me.

PIOTR: You're worried he might do something to harm you.

RAYISHA: It's not what he might do. It's how he thinks.

PIOTR:	Yes that's a mystery, for sure. Vasley is an orphan. A child left to his own devices becomes a man without an anchor. Nobody knows why he thinks or does anything. Including himself probably.

YAKOV is approaching from the distance, carrying a bag of coal.

RAYISHA: Is that Yakov approaching?

PIOTR: Yes...

RAYISHA: Don't force him to do this. He'll resent me.

YAKOV: *(Near now.)* I got the coal. But I think they'll be overcharging you for it.

PIOTR: So if they ever get another horse I'll overcharge them for shoeing it. That's how the system works.

RAYISHA: There could be something wrong with that system.

PIOTR: Well when you get to Petersburg you'll find someone who knows of a better one.

YAKOV: How is she getting to Petersburg?

PIOTR: You're taking her there. And I don't want to see you back here until you've found a safe situation for her.

YAKOV: And if I can't?

PIOTR: Then still don't bother coming back. Because you won't have a job waiting for you.

RAYISHA: *(To YAKOV.)* He doesn't mean that.

YAKOV: I don't care if he does. I don't think I'll come back anyway. I'll get you into a good circumstance, and then I'll find one for myself. If worse comes to worst, we can join the thousands of starving people banging on the gates of the Czar's palace and wait for our dear leader to have his army gun us all down.

PIOTR: That's the spirit. Look on the bright side.

YAKOV: *(Touches RAYISHA's shoulder.)* We'll leave tomorrow. Pack lightly. It's a long walk.

RAYISHA: We're going to walk?

PIOTR: No, I can give you the train fare.

RAYISHA: Oh, that's so generous. Thank you, Piotr.

YAKOV: Yes. Thank you, Piotr.

PIOTR: You're paying your own way.

YAKOV: Of course I am. I don't know what got into me.

> *YAKOV laughs and leaves. RAYISHA hugs PIOTR.*

RAYISHA: I owe you my life.

PIOTR: *(Helping her leave.)* Well let's see how it turns out first.

RAYISHA: No no. I do.

PIOTR: Please stop.

RAYISHA: But I do...

PIOTR: Please... It's too much...

RAYISHA: But...

PIOTR: Shh...

Scene 9

> *Tavern. SASHA has joined VASLEY and MAKAROV at their table. SASHA slowly, arduously takes notes while MAKAROV talks. And VASLEY devours some kind of stew.*

MAKAROV: Our targets are all very much alike. They read the same books. Think and do the same things. They're the most predictably annoying generation we have ever had. They preach liberty without ever considering its dangers. And they have never been able to recognize one undeniable truth. That submission to the law is essential to the survival of man. *(To SASHA.)* Did you get all that?

SASHA: Sort of. And thank you for allowing me to rejoin you.

MAKAROV: Well even if you can't clearly explain the reasons for our actions, you should at least be able to repeat the official jargon.

SASHA: So that I can tell our recruits.

MAKAROV: Or the court where you'll have to defend your actions if things don't go our way. But let's not dwell on that. Tell Vasley here the most important thing you've learned about being an agent for the Department of Safety.

SASHA: Well for one thing, we can't arrest all the subversives, or we'll be out of a job. *(He laughs.)* That was just a joke.

MAKAROV: A stupid joke.

SASHA: Absolutely. *(To VASLEY.)* Forget it immediately.

MAKAROV: *(To VASLEY.)* But even in that stupid joke there's a grain of truth. We won't know when the swamp has been completely drained. So instead of dredging forever, bring the suspects quickly to the surface and into the light of everyday life.

VASLEY: How?

MAKAROV: *(To SASHA.)* Tell him.

SASHA: I could. But it'd be a lot better coming from you.

> *MAKAROV smiles. Pats SASHA on the head.*

MAKAROV: *(To VASLEY.)* Offer your support. We'll provide you with money to give them. Not too much or they'll become suspicious. And always show enthusiasm for their beliefs. That way when you question what they've been up to, it will seem only that you're keen to know more about their cause.

SASHA: That's what I do.

MAKAROV: You mean since you stopped beating and murdering them.

SASHA: I've never mur— *(To VASLEY.)* Well once or twice but that's when I was new at it. And my habits from the past were hard to shake.

MAKAROV: *(To VASLEY.)* He was a criminal. Part of the Streina Boys gang. Every one of them a killer or a thief. We recruited quite a few of them. The more uncivilized ones we eventually had to send off to the camps.

SASHA: And I sure didn't want that happening to me.

MAKAROV: And that's why he worked so hard to get housebroken.

VASLEY: You mean like a dog.

MAKAROV: Exactly like a dog. Anyway the objective is to keep information flowing. For the time being you should stay in the bookshop and get close to the regular customers. That man and woman who were leaving when Sasha showed up...

VASLEY: They're both women. Sisters.

MAKAROV: *(To VASLEY.)* You told me they were—

SASHA: I was sure they were—

VASLEY: One of them wears pants.

MAKAROV: Why?

VASLEY: She's been to Europe.

MAKAROV: Well...besides all that, what did you make of them? Are they just followers? Or are they types that people could be drawn to? Possible leaders.

VASLEY: Maya might be.

SASHA: I bet she's the one in the pants.

VASLEY: Yes. But I don't think it's because of the pants.

SASHA: Explain.

MAKAROV: *(To VASLEY.)* Don't bother. What about the other one?

VASLEY: Olga. I'm not sure about her. When I see her or try talking to her, I get dizzy.

SASHA:	Dizzy? What are you, a child? *(To MAKAROV.)* Dizzy…
VASLEY:	*(To MAKAROV.)* She's…appealing. But so is Maya. And strong. They're both very strong.
MAKAROV:	But you're smitten with Olga. Has she shown any interest in you?
VASLEY:	She finds me annoying.
SASHA:	Everyone probably finds you annoying.
VASLEY:	That's true. But her reason is something I'd rather not talk about.
SASHA:	What is it?
MAKAROV:	He said he doesn't want to talk about it.
SASHA:	He's allowed to do that? There's nothing I won't talk about.
MAKAROV:	You might consider reviewing that policy. I've heard more than enough about your digestive problems, for example. *(To VASLEY.)* Continue.
VASLEY:	Well just when I was starting to be convinced she didn't want any more to do with me, she brought me a new pair of socks. And a few days ago she made me soup.
SASHA:	Sounds like she pities you.
MAKAROV:	Does she?
VASLEY:	Yes. I'm sure that's it.
MAKAROV:	Well pity is better than nothing. Use it. Bring her closer to you. *(Standing.)* Sasha will be your handler.

VASLEY: What's that?

SASHA: Your boss.

MAKAROV: *(To VASLEY.)* Your connection to me. When he contacts you, just report anything you think might be important.

VASLEY: And by important you mean... useful.

MAKAROV: Exactly. *(Extends a hand.)* Welcome to our fraternity.

>   *They shake. MAKAROV leaves.*

SASHA: An impressive man, isn't he?

VASLEY: He has a good voice. And I like the way he sits.

SASHA: What's that mean? The way he sits?

VASLEY: He sits like he doesn't feel weakened by it. I feel at risk whenever I'm not on my feet. Don't you?

SASHA: No. Well maybe. A little. Anyway what did you make of everything he told you?

VASLEY: *(Thinks.)* It made me more hungry.

>   *VASLEY continues to eat his stew.*

>   *SASHA watches him, then checks his notes.*

Scene 10

> *YAKOV and RAYISHA arrive in Petersburg during the Bloody Sunday riot. They are huddled under a tree with mayhem all around them. Shouting, screaming, gunfire, horses on the run. RAYISHA has her head on his chest, cowering.*

RAYISHA: What's going on?! What do you see?!

YAKOV: Horses trampling people. Soldiers shooting in all directions.

RAYISHA: And those explosions!

YAKOV: Bombs. At least two of them. Something has gone very wrong.

RAYISHA: You think we could be killed?

YAKOV: Who knows. Nice welcome, eh!

RAYISHA: What should we do?

YAKOV: Stay here and wait for it to stop, I guess.

RAYISHA: Suppose it doesn't. Suppose it gets worse. What do we do then?

YAKOV: I don't know.

> *An explosion.*

> *They both scream. YAKOV is much louder.*

You shouldn't scream like that. It'll bring attention.

RAYISHA: You screamed too.

YAKOV: I did?

> *Another explosion. YAKOV grabs her and they both fall to their knees. Cowering.*

RAYISHA: This is horrible! What is this!?

YAKOV: I'm not sure! A riot? A strike? An uprising...

Another explosion very near them! RAYISHA screams again.

RAYISHA: You didn't scream that time.

YAKOV: I wanted to.

More gunshots. Other people screaming.

RAYISHA: It sounds like the end of the world!!

YAKOV puts her on his back. They rush off. Smoke. Lots of it.

Fade out on this. A light up on:

VASLEY sitting on his cot. His hands over his ears. Rocking slowly back and forth.

Scene 11

The Bookshop. VASLEY sweeps while the streets erupt in violence, and the MASTER yells at him from above.

MASTER: This is it! I told you this was coming. The people have found out about all the corruption that's been going on. (*Stepping on to the landing.*) They always uncover it eventually no matter what dark corner it's hidden in. Do you remember me saying that!?

VASLEY: No...

MASTER: What!?

VASLEY: No! I don't!!

MASTER: Well do you remember this? The masses will revolt from fear of starvation. The Czar's army will murder them from fear of what they'll do if they're left to starve. That was a prediction. Do you remember me making it. It wasn't that long ago. Well do you remember or not?!

A knock on the door. VASLEY ignores it.

VASLEY: I remember something like that.

MASTER: "Something like that." Mother of Christ! Where's my supper?!

VASLEY: It's too early,

MASTER: Says who. It's not too early if I'm hungry, is it. What are you doing down there anyway?

Another knock.

VASLEY: Sweeping the floor.

MASTER: Oh dear God. The streets are on fire, and you're sweeping the damn floor. You might be too stupid to live through these times.

VASLEY: I was thinking that myself.

MASTER: What?!

VASLEY: You might be right!!

Another very loud knock on the door. And another. VASLEY leaves.

MASTER: What's going on down there now?!

VASLEY comes back. A very angry YAKOV with RAYISHA still on his back follows on.

YAKOV:	What the hell, man! Didn't you hear us knocking?!
VASLEY:	Yes but I was scared. You could have been anyone.
YAKOV:	Some other human beings looking for shelter, you mean! So you're still a pathetic weakling!
VASLEY:	Well under the circumstances... Are you all right, Rayisha?
YAKOV:	Does she look all right? She's scared half to death.
RAYISHA:	Please tell us what's going on out there?
VASLEY:	It's hard to know exactly.
YAKOV:	The soldiers are shooting people!
VASLEY:	Are you sure? Maybe they're just shooting in their general direction. Trying to warn them.
RAYISHA:	Warn them about what?
VASLEY:	That...they need to stop what they're doing.
YAKOV:	And what's so bad about what they're doing? Are they objecting to something?
VASLEY:	Objecting? Do you mean protesting?
YAKOV:	Yes. Yes. Protesting. Are they protesting?
VASLEY:	Yes. Probably.
RAYISHA:	Protesting what?
YAKOV:	Working conditions. Taxation levels. The food supply. I bet it was the food supply. That always gets people going.
RAYISHA:	Is there a food shortage here, Vasley?

VASLEY: Yes. Maybe.

YAKOV: What do you mean maybe? Is there enough food for the people or not. Is this a legitimate protest, or is it just a bunch of people getting together to make noise and cause trouble?

VASLEY: Look, let's none of us ask or answer any more questions, all right. Let's just hope it all stops and we can get back to...whatever we were doing.

YAKOV: You mean sweeping the floor? What's wrong with you?

RAYISHA: People might be getting killed out there.

VASLEY: Well maybe that's better.

YAKOV: Better than what?

VASLEY: Better than having to deal with the pressure some of us are under. Having to deal with making decisions that are just too difficult to make... even under... normal...

                    The MASTER is approaching the landing.

RAYISHA: Who's that coming?

VASLEY: You should leave.

YAKOV: Why?

VASLEY: Just leave.

YAKOV: And go where? We were told you could help us and we—

VASLEY: It's the Master.

YAKOV: The Master? You mean Piotr's cousin?

                    He puts RAYISHA down.

VASLEY:
No. Half-brother. And he'll see her and think she's...

The MASTER enters in a soiled night gown. He looks even more sickly.

MASTER:
This was not supposed to happen until I was long dead! *(Takes a few steps down.)* I can't be subjected to all this in my condition. I provided them with those books on the understanding that nothing too drastic would happen in the near future. A few meetings. The exchange of information. The continued education of the oppressed. And eventually even the army. That would have been enough for now. *(Stops.)* Weren't they aware of the rumours about the positive things the Czar has enacted? Even my female companions have heard them. The latest one in particular should have been encouraging. It's about a new law that grants people the right to not believe in God. If that's not progress, then what the fuck is?! But oh no, there wasn't enough patience. Not enough faith in the ability to transform blind obedience into organized resistance. And this is what we get! *(Notices RAYISHA.)* Well aren't you a sweet young thing?

He starts back up into his room.

(To VASLEY.) Yes. Make sure they're all blind from now on. They won't get so upset when I get too close. Give me a minute or two then send her up. And that man there who brought her. Give him a coin and send him on his way.

He is gone.

VASLEY:
You have to leave. There's no sanctuary here.

YAKOV: Well not for her, there isn't. What have you got yourself into here, Vasley?

RAYISHA: *(To VASLEY.)* Why does he want me to go up there? Does he need some cleaning done?

YAKOV: Oh for godsake. You're in the city now, girl. You can't ask stupid questions like that. *(To VASLEY.)* Even though she has every right to.

            OLGA comes in supporting a wounded MAYA who almost immediately collapses onto the floor.

VASLEY: How'd you get in?

OLGA: The door was unlocked.

MAYA: You better go see to that.

VASLEY: What?

            VASLEY is trying to bring OLGA into focus.

OLGA: Vasley! What are you doing? Stop blinking at me like that and go make sure the door is locked!

VASLEY: Yes. I can do that!

            He runs off.

MAYA: *(To YAKOV.)* Quite a night, eh.

OLGA: Were you in the rear of the crowd?

YAKOV: No. We just arrived.

OLGA: Too late though.

MAYA: *(Trying to breathe.)* The starting time was clearly marked in the pamphlet we provided.

RAYISHA: He meant we just arrived in the city.

MAYA: Oh well then...welcome. Hope you enjoy your stay. It's usually not so noisy, but...

She is trying to steady her breaths.

YAKOV: *(To OLGA.)* Why is he having trouble breathing?

MAYA: Her. I'm a...her.

OLGA: And she's been shot.

MAYA: Somewhere near my...shoulder. It's not too bad. I think I might be in shock though.

OLGA is looking at RAYISHA more closely. VASLEY returns.

OLGA: She's blind?

YAKOV: Yeah.

OLGA: Well this is no place for someone who's... defective.

YAKOV: Don't call her that.

MAYA: He's right. It sounds harsh.

OLGA: It'll be a lot harsher if she finds herself in the middle of that insanity out there.

VASLEY: Good point. But...it actually does sound better out there now. So you can probably leave.

OLGA: Who?

VASLEY: *(Trying not to look at her.)* All of you. Yes. Even you. I mean I need you all to leave. Because these are complex issues. The issues out there. And I need time...to think about them.

OLGA: What's there to think about? The army and the police are attacking people.

VASLEY: Unless they were provoked.

OLGA: They weren't.

MAYA: Their mere presence was a provocation to the protesters though.

VASLEY: I see. Yes. Well if the army provoked the protesters and they in turn provoked the army to shoot at them. Then, of course, that would be something else. Unless, I mean even so...some of us need to eat. And a place to sleep. And too much unrest might mean—

YAKOV: What are you talking about?

VASLEY: I'll need time to find an answer to that. Right now you all have to leave.

OLGA: (*Off MAYA.*) But she's injured!

YAKOV: And we have nowhere else to go.

MAYA: No he's right. We'll compromise him if we're found here.

VASLEY: What's that mean? Compromise me with who? About what? I just meant... I mean, I really just meant that... have tasks to perform. And a meal to prepare.

MAYA: Of course. And it does seem quieter out there, so... (*To OLGA.*) We can probably make it home.

OLGA: All right. But... (*Off RAYISHA.*) We're taking her with us.

MAYA: Definitely. We can't leave her to that decrepit bastard upstairs.

OLGA:	*(To YAKOV.)* You disgust us.
YAKOV:	Why? Oh. No, she's not... I'm not...
OLGA:	*(To YAKOV.)* How many more like her do you have working for you?
YAKOV:	Working for me? No—
OLGA:	*(To VASLEY.)* And are they all going to be blind or maimed from now on?
VASLEY:	No I'll put my foot down about that.

OLGA starts off, leading RAYISHA.

RAYISHA:	Yakov?
YAKOV:	Go with them. They have a home to go to. That's not something to turn your back on.
MAYA:	*(To YAKOV.)* You can come too if you want.
OLGA:	Maya. Please. He's a pimp.
MAYA:	*(To OLGA.)* So can't pimps be reformed? *(To YAKOV.)* Please. Come along.

OLGA helps MAYA out.

YAKOV:	Okay. Sure. But let's get something straight. I'm not a—

But they are gone.

(To VASLEY.) Who are they anyway? How do you know them?

VASLEY:	I'm not prepared to answer those questions because of the possible consequences.
YAKOV:	Who from?

VASLEY: Everyone. Now just leave before they get too
                   far ahead, and you lose them. They're your
                   only chance of sleeping indoors tonight.

                   YAKOV hesitates.

                   Leave!

                   YAKOV hurries off.

                   (Sits on his cot.) I need time to think. About
                   what to do. Or not do. Or not even think
                   about doing... Then there are the questions.
                   Not just other people's questions but my
                   own. *(Stands.)* Why do I need to know who
                   was provoked or not provoked, who reads
                   these books, or who follows what these books
                   say to do. I've already been told what to
                   think and do about all that. And by someone
                   who's willing to pay me for thinking and
                   doing it. Or for not thinking and still doing
                   it. *(Sits again.)* Yes. Right. Good... I mean good
                   enough. For now. I hope.

Scene 12

                   *OLGA, MAYA, and RAYISHA hurry
                   on, but pause to give MAYA a rest. But
                   YAKOV is right behind them.*

YAKOV: No don't stop!

MAYA: *(Collapses on the ground.)* Just a few minutes.

OLGA: I need to look at her wound.

RAYISHA: Look to see if the bullet went all the way
                   through.

OLGA:	Yes... Right. (*Looking.*) It did.
	OLGA takes off her scarf to staunch the flow of MAYA's blood.
RAYISHA:	Good. Then there's less chance it will fester.
YAKOV:	(*To OLGA.*) She and her mother helped with these things back home.
RAYISHA:	When the idiot village boys accidently shot each other while hunting. (*To YAKOV.*) You wounded two of your friends, didn't you.
YAKOV:	Just trying to get them before they got me.
	YAKOV and MAYA both laugh.
OLGA:	Oh for godsake.
MAYA:	Come on. That was funny.
OLGA:	(*To YAKOV.*) So you're from the same village. Is that where you get most of the girls for that monster.
YAKOV:	There you go again. You've got that all wrong.
RAYISHA:	He's who Piotr told us to go to for help.
MAYA:	So you came here for shelter, and you found yourself in the middle of a slaughter.
RAYISHA:	A slaughter. It was that bad?
MAYA:	It started out well enough. We were trying to warn the government what would happen—
OLGA:	If they didn't make changes.
MAYA:	We thought if they saw how much support we had it might bring them to their senses. But as usual—

OLGA: They proved how ignorant and selfish they are not to care. They're going to need a very strong taste of what they've been dishing out.

MAYA: The march was led by one of the few priests who's not owned by the government. He was arrested almost immediately.

OLGA: He'll be tortured then murdered. And there are a lot of us who will want revenge.

MAYA: She means justice.

OLGA: But first revenge.

YAKOV: When you say "a lot of us..."

MAYA: She means people who care about people like you.

YAKOV: When you say "people like you..."

RAYISHA: She means people who don't have very much. They want to help us.

YAKOV: Good. What I need help with most is finding a job.

RAYISHA: And I'm afraid of starving to death on the street.

OLGA: Of course you are. We can help you both.

An explosion.

MAYA: She means we can try.

More rifle shots.

MAYA starts off. Supported by OLGA.

But right now I need to get to our house, and lie down in my bed.

YAKOV and RAYISHA follow.

YAKOV: She has a bed. A real bed.

                    Sounds of people approaching quickly.
                    More loud shots.

MAYA: We better hurry. They're probably trying to
                    round up stragglers.

                    They start running. Gunshots over their
                    heads.

YAKOV: *(Ducking.)* That one went just by my ear.
                    (Turning.) Bastards!! *(Running, with the rest.)*
                    They're soldiers. They should be protecting
                    us. Not trying to kill us, right.

MAYA: In theory.

                    They are all off.

Scene 12A

                    PIOTR comes on holding a letter.

PIOTR: *(With excitement.)* A letter from someone
                    in Petersburg who thinks he's my brother.
                    I've had to gather you together to hear it
                    because most of you were too goddamn lazy
                    to learn how to read. *(Reading.)* There has
                    been an uprising. Our side lost. Something
                    I knew would happen if desperation caused
                    people to move too recklessly. But there
                    the idiots were. Marching down the street
                    yelling out their stupid slogans when the
                    Czar's mounted soldiers tore into the crowd
                    without mercy. Mercy. That's a word which
                    will be meaningless in our country forever.

Hundreds killed. Many more injured. And I'm sure there's more to come from both sides. As for Vasley, he still can't decide if he should let his brain or his asshole do his thinking for him. But even he must be worried that the future will be very bleak and dangerous. *(To the assembled.)* And so should all of us!

He leaves.

Scene 13

Tavern. VASLEY in new pants and shirt, waits alone. Just staring at the drink in front of him.

A loud exchange of voices from somewhere in the tavern. It's over fast, but it has put VASLEY on edge.

YAKOV enters in a factory worker's jacket.

YAKOV: There you are. Your Master gave you my note then.

VASLEY: No, he threw it out. I found it in the trash.

YAKOV: Good for you. *(Sitting.)* It's been some time, eh. I see we both have new clothing.

VASLEY: Yes. I have a paying job now.

YAKOV: A job which requires you to look presentable.

VASLEY: And you found work in a munitions factory.

YAKOV: You knew that?

VASLEY: I saw you entering the factory.

YAKOV: Because you just happened to be there.

They just look at each other.

VASLEY: I was watching. I'm with the Department of Safety.

YAKOV: You're a spy?

VASLEY: No I'm just someone who watches and reports to actual spies.

YAKOV: And now you're reporting on the factory?

VASLEY: I'm looking for signs that there could be more of what happened that bloody Sunday.

YAKOV: More of the army shooting people and trampling them with their horses.

VASLEY: More of the things that brought that on. Bad feelings about the Czar. Have you noticed any of that in the factory?

YAKOV: I've noticed plenty of that. Is that why we're meeting? Do you want names?

VASLEY: Are you willing to provide them?

YAKOV: Do you pay for information like that? Because I'll need the money in advance.

VASLEY: You mean right now? I only have so much on me.

YAKOV: Well whatever you have, I'll take.

> *VASLEY produces some money. Hands it over.*

VASLEY: Also, those sisters you met at the bookshop, I believe you're still in touch with them.

YAKOV: So you've been watching them too.

VASLEY: But only from a healthy distance.

YAKOV: What's that mean? A healthy distance.

VASLEY: Well there are...certain feelings that I need to keep under control. I can't tell you what they are.

YAKOV: I think I can guess. You're a sad little creature, aren't you?

VASLEY: Yes. I suppose I am. But anyway, I'll need you to keep me informed about their activities.

YAKOV: Whatever you say. So I'll be a spy too. Two orphans helping out the Czar. Who would have thought?

VASLEY: They did. The Czar's people target orphans to work for them because we don't have the support that allows us to say no.

YAKOV: Hmm. Vasley Klimkov has an intelligent thought. And he expresses it clearly. So do you enjoy the same things the people you work for do. Do you enjoy the opera, for example?

VASLEY: The opera?

YAKOV: Yes. That large fancy place where people sing loudly in a foreign language.

VASLEY: Things like that are for everyone, Yakov.

YAKOV: The hell they are!! What about fresh fruit? You must get plenty of that. Or do the Czar, and his good for nothing family, keep most of it for themselves?

VASLEY: Well I don't eat very much, so—

YAKOV: That's not the point. Do you want me to tell you what my point is?

VASLEY: Well now that you're receiving government money from me you shouldn't actually have a point. Unless it's the same as the government's.

YAKOV: Not even about fresh fruit, or the opera?

VASLEY: Well even then I'd have to decide if that point was one the government would agree with.

YAKOV: And if you decided that it wouldn't, you'd have to report the people who made the point. Whatever it was.

VASLEY: Well they pay me. And they're much more organized. And stronger.

YAKOV: For the moment at least. So you're a coward who's just doing your job out of fear.

VASLEY: Well what else could I be, or do, when I have no defences.

YAKOV: You could do nothing! Just hide from your superiors. Offer them no assistance.

VASLEY: Can someone do that with the... other side?

YAKOV: The people, Vasley. The other side are the people that you spy on.

VASLEY: So with that point of view I take it that you're not actually willing to join me. So that was all a game for you?

YAKOV: A game. A test. The money was a little bonus. Yes I'm fully committed to the rebellion. Always have been, I think. Even before I knew there was one.

YAKOV stands, takes off his jacket, rolls up his sleeves.

Where do you want this to happen?

VASLEY: You're planning to beat me.

YAKOV: It's been quite a while. I'm sure you must have missed it. So right here? Or outside?

VASLEY: It won't change my mind.

YAKOV: I'm not interested in changing your mind. I want to break your back.

VASLEY: I'm sorry. I can't let that happen. Just the thought of it is making me ill. So... *(Taking out a pistol.)* I'll have to rely on this. They insisted I carry one.

YAKOV looks at him.

YAKOV: You might have to pay for what you're doing to our world. Your bosses won't survive.

VASLEY: I think that's possible, yes.

YAKOV: Well whatever happens... Good luck to us both.

VASLEY: How's Rayisha doing?

YAKOV: She's being taken care of. I'll pass on your regards.

VASLEY: My regards. Yes. Do that.

YAKOV shakes his head, smiles sadly. Picks up his jacket. Leaves.

VASLEY looks at his gun.

Scene 14

> MAKAROV *is behind his desk at the Department of Safety, reading a report. There is a portrait of the Czar suspended in the air.*
>
> SASHA *enters.* MAKAROV *continues to read without acknowledging his presence.* SASHA *clears his throat. Again. Same result.*

SASHA: Sir... *(No response.)* Sir... I'm here, sir.

MAKAROV: *(Looking up.)* Yes you are. Have you compiled your list?

SASHA: Yes, sir. Thirty-eight names with addresses. Twice as many as any of my colleagues.

MAKAROV: It's not a competition, Sasha.

SASHA: No disrespect, sir, but I'm pretty sure it is.

MAKAROV: Then let's just say that it's not a competition you're favoured to win. There are factors which don't you help your case. Your mental instability, for example.

SASHA: That's a product of my abandonment and the harshness of my childhood, as you know. And I'm working on it.

MAKAROV: Well don't work too hard. It might not be something you can overcome. Tonight's raids will be a major challenge.

SASHA: So I'll be in charge then.

MAKAROV: As much as you ever are, yes. Where's Klimkov?

SASHA:	I don't know. Maybe he's run away. So many of us have. Run off. Or switched to the other side. And Klimkov isn't the most reliable person.
MAKAROV:	Don't be fooled by the fact that he appears to be in a constant stupor. He has qualities he keeps hidden. As for changing sides, he's too cautious to expose himself to the dangers those desperate people are in.

VASLEY enters.

And there he is now.

VASLEY:	Sir?
MAKAROV:	We were wondering if you'd deserted us to join the rabble.
VASLEY:	I thought about it, but I wasn't sure how to make the approach.
MAKAROV:	A joke. Good for you. *(To SASHA.)* Be careful with this one. He's feeling his oats.

VASLEY hands MAKAROV a few pieces of paper.

How many?

VASLEY:	Sixty-three. That includes the dozen that are usually at the meetings Olga and Maya have every night. *(To SASHA.)* They're the sister graduate students.
SASHA:	I know who they are. I shot one of them.
MAKAROV:	For no good reason.
SASHA:	She was yelling obscenities about the Czar.

MAKAROV: Everyone in Russia has at one time yelled an obscenity about the Czar. *(To VASLEY.)* And your friend at the factory?

SASHA: We can grab him tonight. He works the late shift.

VASLEY: You're sure about that?

SASHA: *(To MAKAROV.)* He thinks he's the only one who's been watching.

MAKAROV: We've had a half dozen men on it. That factory has too many people coming and going when it should just be closed because of the strike. They're making something.

SASHA: I suspect bombs.

MAKAROV: Based on what?

VASLEY: He always suspects bombs.

MAKAROV: And why not rifles, Sasha? Or even pistols.

SASHA: *(Scoffing.)* Pistols... *(Immediately regretful.)* Sorry...

VASLEY: *(To MAKAROV.)* It's rifles. I got a look inside.

MAKAROV: Good for you. All right... *(Standing.)* Here's the situation. Tonight, if this roundup is handled well, we could set their movement back on its heels. Many of the people we're arresting will be very hard to replace. But if we fail and they find themselves in a position to make some demands, very soon after that there will be a constitution. And that constitution will guarantee that sweeping reforms occur. Those reforms, I guarantee you, will not be good for feeble-minded fools... *(To SASHA.)*

...like you. *(To both.)* You will be put away in a prison or... *(To SASHA.)* ...in an asylum... *(To both.)* ...and never be heard from again. So get the job done. You're fighting to maintain the status quo. And therefore, your actual survival. Sasha, you can go.

SASHA hesitates. Looks at each of them.

I said go. Get your people prepared.

SASHA leaves.

(Standing.) Vasley. Have you made plans?

VASLEY: Sir?

MAKAROV: For what you'll do if things don't go our way. Not all the people love our Great Czar.

VASLEY: That's true. Many of them think he's an idiot and a criminal.

MAKAROV: And do you agree with them?

VASLEY: Do you?

MAKAROV: Of course. All you have to do is listen to what he says. It's a miracle he's lasted this long. Anyway... *(To audience.)* I'm off to the Argentine. I think I'll feel safer there win or lose in the short term. Fresh air. A moderate climate. A good place to relax and just fade away. The people could very well prevail eventually. They possess a desperate bravery. *(To VASLEY.)* Make plans for yourself, just in case...

VASLEY nods and starts out.

Oh. And keep a close eye on Sasha tonight. I'd like most of the people we arrest to arrive at the jail alive.

VASLEY nods and leaves. MAKAROV watches him go.

(*To audience.*) I have a weak spot for the young fellow. I'm not sure why. I had a dog once. I was always having to tell people he was much smarter than they gave him credit for. Sometimes the dog proved me right. Other times he just begged for food. But at least he did it with a certain amount of dignity.

Lights change.

SASHA and VASLEY, both in a hurry, come face to face on the streets.

SASHA: You better watch yourself tonight, pal. I've got instructions to keep an eye on you.

VASLEY: I've got instructions to keep an eye you.

SASHA: (*Grabs VASLEY's ear.*) Hey, don't fool around. Your position is not as secure as you think.

VASLEY: Neither is yours.

SASHA: (*Pulls the ear harder.*) I told you not to fool around! You should have brought those sisters in a long time ago. If I see you trying to help them escape I'll put a bullet in your head.

VASLEY: (*Breaking away.*) Thank you for the warning.

SASHA watches him go.

SASHA: (*Yelling after him.*) It wasn't a warning! It was a threat!!

He starts off in the other direction. Stops. Thinks. And runs off to follow VASLEY.

Scene 15

> *Darkness. VASLEY and YAKOV are on the run, but VASLEY keeps stumbling. Several men are after them. Lots of shouting and instructions in the near distance.*

YAKOV: For godsake. Try to stay on your feet.

VASLEY: Sorry. I was never taught how to run properly.

YAKOV: It's not something you need to be— *(Picking him up again.)* Okay this won't work. We have to hide. Quickly, under this bridge.

> *They duck down. A crowd of invisible noisy men pass by.*

            All that just for me? What did you tell them?

VASLEY: That you were smart.

YAKOV: And that's a crime now, is it?

VASLEY: Well a lot of men ran from that factory, so they're after them too.

YAKOV: They ran because they were scared.

VASLEY: They ran because they were making rifles.

YAKOV: Yes. For the army.

VASLEY: For the army? Not for the rebellion? Is that why you're not on strike?

YAKOV: Yes. Three officers showed up and threatened to shoot us all if we didn't keep working.

VASLEY: They couldn't do that without authorization.

YAKOV: Well they seemed authorized to me. And your spy bosses don't know that's why the factory is still open?

VASLEY:	No. The army must have plans to attack the bureaucracy as well.
YAKOV:	As well as who else?
VASLEY:	I'm told that in the new environment many different factions will be vying for power. It's already dangerous for people like me.
YAKOV:	So why'd you put yourself at risk to come save me?
VASLEY:	It wasn't really for you. It might be safe to move now.

They stand and move out.

	It was for Rayisha. If Olga and her sister are arrested tonight, Rayisha will need someone to take care of her.
YAKOV:	If you knew they could be arrested, why didn't you warn them?
VASLEY:	I couldn't. They're being watched.

They look around and proceed cautiously.

YAKOV:	So they'll be thrown in prison, and that's it for them, eh.
VASLEY:	Well Maya will probably lead any insurrection, but I might be able to save Olga. If I can do that, I'll take her and Rayisha both back to the village. Piotr sent a letter to tell me that his wife killed herself.
YAKOV / VASLEY:	Finally!
VASLEY:	Yes. So he'll be able to take Rayisha into his house now.
YAKOV:	And what will Olga do?

VASLEY: *(Looking out and up.)* Olga is a dream that must stay alive.

YAKOV: What?

VASLEY: Can you do this or not?

YAKOV: Yes. I can.

> *SASHA steps out of the darkness ahead of them. Gun out and pointed at them.*

SASHA: I told you I'd be keeping an eye on you. So you have gone over to the rabble.

VASLEY: No. I captured him.

YAKOV: Yes he beat me and took me prisoner. Doesn't look like he's got it in him, does he.

> *VASLEY looks at him.*

SASHA: No. It doesn't!

YAKOV: Well in that case...

> *YAKOV puts his hand up and appears to be surrendering when he suddenly lunges for SASHA. SASHA shoots him. YAKOV falls to his knees. Reaches for VASLEY.*

(In pain.) Oh... That was a mistake. *(Reaches for VASLEY.)* Help me up... will you.

> *VASLEY extends his hand, but YAKOV falls all the way over. Dead. VASLEY kneels beside the body.*

VASLEY: He's dead. The boss told us he wanted people taken alive. He isn't going to like this.

SASHA: He's not going to find out about it. *(Approaches VASLEY.)* I'm going to enjoy this next part very much.

VASLEY: Maybe not.

                *Very quickly VASLEY lifts the gun that he
                managed to take out a bit earlier without
                being seen and shoots SASHA. SASHA
                staggers back a bit, clutching his chest...*

SASHA: God I hate you... so much.

                He falls. Dead.

                *VASLEY stands. Looks down at both
                bodies. Lingering over YAKOV.*

VASLEY: I'm sorry.

                He runs off.

Scene 16

                *MAKAROV's office. MAKAROV behind
                his desk. MAYA, in restraints, stands in
                front of him.*

MAYA: Why aren't I in jail with my sister?

MAKAROV: Your sister's not in jail. She escaped.

MAYA: So you had her killed then?

MAKAROV: Is that what the word "escaped" means to
                you? *(Off her look.)* She got clean away. It was
                our friend Vasley's doing. He took her into
                his personal custody and she never appeared
                that night again. You never know when your
                heart is going to get the best of you, right.
                Anyway, we don't know where she is.

                He stands.

MAYA:
And you won't get any help from me in finding her. Olga or anyone else. The people you've rounded up tonight are all you're going to get. The rest will go underground and keep planning to overthrow you all. So go ahead. Torture me. You'll get nothing from me!

MAKAROV:
I believe you. No need to pound your chest about it. I'm just curious about a couple of things. What exactly did you want from the people you were trying to influence with all your knowledge and opinions.

MAYA:
Want from them?

MAKAROV:
You must have expected them to give you something. Or were you just satisfied with having an adoring audience?

MAYA:
We expected them to foment revolution.

MAKAROV:
Yes yes. Revolution. Kill the Czar and all that. But in the meantime. On a more personal, even emotional level, what did you want?

MAYA:
(Looks at him.) We "wanted" them to bind themselves to each other. And to believe in a future where life is better for everyone who needs and deserves one.

MAKAROV:
"Deserves" is an odd word to use. Just curious, do you think people deserve to be rewarded just for existing?

MAYA:
For just existing? No. For enduring? Yes. Absolutely.

MAKAROV:
All right. I acknowledge the difference. *(Smiles.)* Well... I'm glad we cleared that up. This is not the time for misunderstandings of any kind.

> *He undoes her restraints. She seems uncertain about why.*

(Sitting again.) I've been told that at your meetings you handed out books. Very long books.

MAYA: Books of instruction and comfort.

MAKAROV: Comfort.

MAYA: Knowledge is comfort. Knowing how things work and what they mean, can make you feel less uncertain about your life.

MAKAROV: Yes. But why did the books have to be so long? Wouldn't a pamphlet have sufficed. One that clearly outlined your beliefs and objectives. I assume these people only had so much time on their hands. They had jobs, didn't they? Or were they all from well-off families like you?

> *He stands, turns partially to the audience.*

(To both MAYA and at times the audience.) Although I might just be thinking about those great novels of ours. So very long. By the time I was in the middle of one I'd forgotten the beginning. And by the end I'd forgotten both the beginning and the middle. And all that was left was the sentiment. *(Turning back to MAYA.)* In our great Russian novels the sentiment is almost unbearable.

MAYA: That's because those novels carry within them the centuries old burden of the peasants and the crimes of the aristocracy.

MAKAROV: I never got that. I just got depressed.

MAYA: Perhaps because you stopped thinking for yourself when you swore blind allegiance to the Czar.

                 He picks up a briefcase from the floor next to his chair.

MAKAROV: *(Casually approaching her.)* If only that were true. Anyway it's been good chatting. And as for throwing you in jail... The way things are going, you'd probably be out in no time. So...

MAYA: What does that mean? I can leave?

MAKAROV: Yes. Or you can stay. *(Gestures.)* Sit. *(Off his look.)* Sit in my chair. Take my desk. Take my position. I'm leaving. So you do the job. See if you can reconcile the state's desire to maintain public order with the overwhelming needs of the people. It might prove harder than you think. Especially now that the people are "binding" themselves together. *(He starts off.)* I'm off to the Argentine. But I wish you luck.

                 MAKAROV leaves. MAYA watches him go then turns her attention to the desk. Makes a slight movement towards it. Hesitates. Then sits in the chair. Thinks.

Scene 17

The MASTER is searching for a book in the much messier piles now on the floor from being spilled at various times. He looks worse than ever and can barely move.

MASTER: What a fucking mess. But when you don't know what you're looking for that doesn't really matter, does it. Just need something special for my last read. Wish I'd taken in more erotica. I'd like to have one more glorious erection before passing. I also wish... No don't start with all that..."if only" and "what could have been" bilge... Just stick to what is real. To have changed a life I would have had to have a life.

VASLEY enters. Dirty and worn out.

MASTER: You're back. Why?

VASLEY: Nowhere else to go.

MASTER: Your career as a spy is over I take it. The people you betrayed will probably hang you, you know.

VASLEY: I betrayed everyone.

MASTER: *(Starting up the stairs.)* Well that's an accomplishment. But I'm talking specifically about the people you spied on. They'll string you up for sure. Not right away. They'll be busy hanging people much more important than you are. But they'll get to you eventually. Try to accept your fate and get on with whatever is left of your worthless life. It's not all your fault. You didn't get much guidance along the way. Not from me, anyway.

VASLEY: That's true.

MASTER: Well I was already on my last legs when you showed up, so what did you expect.

VASLEY: I expected nothing.

MASTER: Yes, that was very apparent. *(Starting off.)* Oh. That blind girl. I heard from Piotr that she made it home all right. So there's that... *(Stops.)* In case you've been worried about her. *(No response.)* Well anyway...

       He starts up again.

       We hear the MASTER's voice as he makes it to the landing and starts into the darkness.

MASTER: You better start thinking about what you'll make for supper. I'm not dead yet! Did you hear me?!

VASLEY: Yes...

MASTER: What!?

VASLEY: Yes!

       He stands slowly, looks around. Sits again. Suddenly stands.

       (To himself.) What about Olga? *(After MASTER.)* Did you hear if Olga is all right!?

MASTER: *(Off.)* Who the hell is she?!

       VASLEY sits again. Head in hands.

Scene 18

The village. RAYISHA on a bench. OLGA looking around.

OLGA: Will you be safe in this place?

RAYISHA: Piotr will take care of me.

OLGA: And when he dies?

RAYISHA: Well if there's no one else, there's always the forest.

OLGA: You'll live in the forest? *(Joining her.)* How will that be possible?

RAYISHA: It won't. But don't concern yourself with me. No one expected me to live this long.

OLGA: The uprising probably failed. I can't go back to the city until I hear it's safe. And if I don't concern myself with your well-being, I won't have much of a purpose in life, will I?

PIOTR comes on with a letter in his hand.

PIOTR: A letter from Vasley... *(To RAYISHA.)* Bad news. Yakov is dead.

RAYISHA lowers her head.

OLGA: How?

PIOTR: The police. He got caught in the same roundup Vasley saved you from. He resisted and...

OLGA: They murdered him... Any word about my sister?

PIOTR: Yes he goes on about that for a while. *(Hands her the letter.)* Here... And thank you for bringing her back.

OLGA:	She's my friend.
PIOTR:	Is that so?
RAYISHA:	Yes. And we should let her stay with us for a while.
PIOTR:	Of course. For as long as she needs. We can't offer her much in the way of accommodation.
RAYISHA:	We've been sleeping in ditches and fields all the way here.
OLGA:	I don't require luxury of any kind. I just want time to get my thoughts in order. In the meantime I can help out in any way you need.
RAYISHA:	Not in the house. That would be a waste. She can teach people in the village how to read.
PIOTR:	I've tried to do that myself since the school closed. Tried to give the young and the old a little knowledge about the world out there. They don't care about those things though. *(Leaving.)* It's so fucking depressing.

OLGA turns to RAYISHA.

OLGA:	What do you think?
RAYISHA:	I think you can make them care.

OLGA takes her hand.

OLGA:	Do you want to hear Vasley's letter?
RAYISHA:	Please.
OLGA:	*(Reading.)* Tell Olga, if she is still there, that there is interesting, even startling news, about her sister. Apparently...

Lights here slowly fade and a light on....

VASLEY on his cot, surrounded by books, composing a letter in a notepad.

OLGA /
VASLEY: She was offered a job in the Czar's secret
                police.

                *OLGA and RAYISHA stand and start off.
                OLGA is still reading, but now her voice
                is fading.*

VASLEY: (*As he writes.*) And not just any job. The
                rumour is that she was actually in charge
                until it was discovered who she really was.
                People think that's bizarre, but I think it's just
                a normal bureaucratic mistake. After the truth
                about her was discovered she was arrested,
                but let out almost immediately because of
                having done such a fine and humane job in
                the two weeks she was in command. There's
                another rumour that she was able to find and
                destroy many incriminating files on you and
                your friends during her time there.

                I myself think that's just wishful thinking.
                Anyway she is probably on her way there to
                you now, so tell Olga that. Give her my kind
                regards and also my best thoughts to Rayisha
                as well. As for me...

                MASTER calls from upstairs.

MASTER: Where's...my...supper!? You hear me, you
                worthless piece of shit!? I'm hungry. And I
                want my supper.

VASLEY: Is that man never going to die?

MASTER: I want my supper!

VASLEY: (*Looks up.*) Make it yourself!!

                He smiles very slightly.

                The end.